LONDON'S NORTHERN HEIGHTS
The H~~

The **Hampste**~~ ~~iles long, connec~~ ~~via **Hampstead** ~~

No other par~~ ~~**~~~~ern Heights** for ~~ ~~pen spaces and associations with famous people. The Trail passes **500 points of interest** – one every fifty yards.

The Trail is divided into **five sections**. Each section starts and ends at a point easily reached by **public transport** and served by **pubs and cafés**. Though each section makes a good walk in its own right, sections can be **easily split** to create less demanding itineraries.

Hampstead has been a cradle of liberal opinion for over two hundred years. No other part of London has exercised such an attraction to thinkers, artists, reformers and campaigners.

Likewise no other transect of London illustrates so many different **styles of architecture**. The Trail passes London's most celebrated example of **Regency** town planning, many superb examples of late **Georgian** terraces and early Victorian **Italianate** villas as well as pockets of innovative **Social Housing** and **International Modernism**.

Hampstead Village has its own eclectic mixture of styles. Beyond Hampstead the route crosses **Hampstead Heath** and passes through one of the world's most influential examples of early 20th century town planning, Dame Henrietta Barnett and Sir Raymond Unwin's Arts and Crafts **Hampstead Garden Suburb**. The last section passes through London's finest surviving concentration of **Edwardian** domestic, retail and ecclesiastical architecture.

The five richly illustrated guides contain **detailed route maps**, a description of every **point of interest** along the route and information on the use of **public transport** to reach the start point and return from the end point of each section.

The route and its documentation have been devised by **The Highgate Society** in collaboration with the **Heath & Hampstead Society**, the **Hampstead Garden Suburb Trust** and the **Hornsey Historical Society**. The information was correct as of May 2012.

A companion trail to the **Hampstead Heritage Trail** is the five section **Northern Heights Circular Walk**. This takes in a further 350 points of interest along its nine mile route through **Highgate Village, Hampstead** and **Hampstead Heath**.

SECTION C
Hampstead to Temple Fortune

Hampstead • The Spaniards • Heath Extension
St Jude's-on-the-Hill • Temple Fortune

Planning your trip

The walk starts at **Hampstead** Underground station and ends at **Temple Fortune**, the shopping centre on the road between Golders Green and Finchley Central.

Allow **three hours** to complete the walk. Walking time is around one hour and a half. The walk is 3.1 miles long. You can shorten the walk by returning by bus from the **Old Bull and Bush**, half way along the route.

Though much of the walk is on paved surfaces the middle section across the Hampstead Heath Extension can be very **muddy** in wet weather. Hampstead Garden Suburb is at its best in late April and early May but the walk should be enjoyable at any time of year when the air is clear and when it is dry underfoot.

It is best to start this section of the trail at Hampstead. You can then appreciate the views of the "Suburb", the name it is known by, as you approach it from the Heath Extension, an important element in its design. This way you also walk mostly **downhill**.

During the middle section you may need to refer to the text and map quite regularly to avoid getting lost.

Facilities

Hampstead offers no shortage of places to **eat and drink**. The Holly Bush Tavern shortly after you start and The Old Bull and Bush, half way along the route at North End, are pleasant places to stop en route. Temple Fortune supports a Costa and Starbucks, both of them close to the Temple Fortune Lane bus stop where you can catch the bus back to Golders Green station. Din and Delisserie are two of a selection of good independent cafés and snack bars on either side of the main road, some of them open seven days a week.

Public conveniences are located in the Heath Extension.

Points of interest: Hampstead Underground station to Whitestone Pond

Reaching Hampstead

From the West End or the City take a Northern Line train showing the destination **Edgware** (not High Barnet or Mill Hill East) to Hampstead Underground station. Hampstead is the third stop after Camden Town.

Journey time from Oxford Circus should be around 35 minutes.

Returning from Temple Fortune

From Temple Fortune take buses 82, 102 or 460 from the Hampstead Way side of the road at stop TE, just south of **Temple Fortune Lane**. After two thirds of a mile get off at Golders Green Underground station – the stop is beneath the railway bridge.

Golders Green, like Hampstead, is on the **Edgware** branch of the Northern line. Trains leave approximately every three minutes as far as Camden Town where the route divides, some trains serving the City, others serving stops in the West End as far as Charing Cross. To return to the start of the walk you can alight at the next stop, Hampstead.

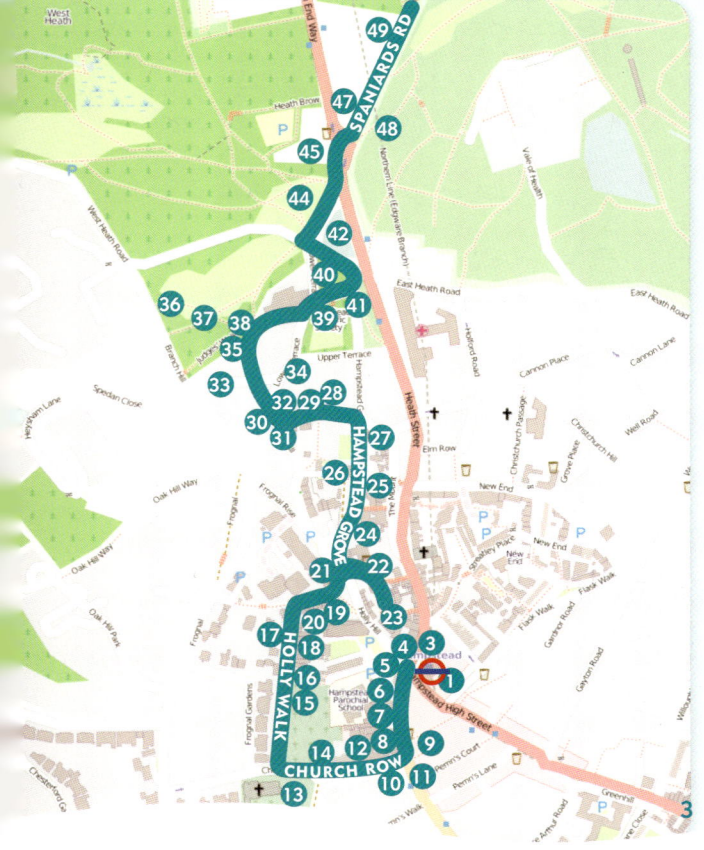

The Walk

Entrance to Hampstead Underground station

*This section of the **Hampstead Trail** covers parts of Hampstead's historic core before climbing to **Whitestone Pond**, the highest point in inner London. It then winds downhill through **Sandy Heath**, a little visited part of Hampstead Heath, before entering Hampstead Garden Suburb through **The Great Wall** at Sunshine Corner.*

*Conceived by **Dame Henrietta Barnett** (1851-1936) and laid out by **Raymond Unwin** (1863-1940) and other celebrated practitioners of urban planning, the Suburb was the source of many innovations in house design characteristic of the period between 1907 and 1939 and an inspiration for **planners** at home and abroad.*

*Despite the quality of its architecture the Suburb was intended to be more than an architectural showpiece. It was designed to offer a new and more **convivial** form of living, catering for the social and recreational needs of its new residents and laid out in a way which would stimulate community **cohesion**.*

1 If you take the underground to reach the start of the walk at Hampstead Underground station you will have been carried up the **tallest lift shafts** on the underground network – unless that is you climb the 300 steps from platform level. By contrast the lifts at Chalk Farm, the shallowest, go down only 21 feet. Designed by Leslie Green, the station was opened by David Lloyd George in 1907. Your exit is at the busy traffic hub of Hampstead, where the High Street crosses Heath Street and Holly Hill.

2 By the 16th century Hampstead's clean air and fresh water attracted successful city merchants who bought or built houses with substantial grounds. Around 1700 the presence of **spa waters** transformed a quiet village into a thriving destination for London pleasure seekers.

3 Across Heath Street from the exit from the underground are the offices of the Nationwide Building Society, located in what, from when it opened in 1874 until 1915, was Hampstead's **fire station**. Its architect was George Vulliamy. Note the water tower from which an alarm alerted firemen of a blaze. A similar tower exists in Highgate Village (Circular Walk, section one). Originally the tower had a gabled roof. The Heath & Hampstead Society is campaigning to have this roof reinstated.

The former Hampstead Fire Station

4 Cross into Heath Street and leave **Oxfam Books**, which stocks a good selection of local guides, on your right.

Moulded brickwork above Nationwide Building Society

Terracotta above shop at corner of Holly Hill

5 The first turning on the right leads to **The Everyman**, a former drill hall which, when converted to a theatre, became a mecca for Hampstead's liberal intelligentsia. Now it is a cinema. According to Gerald Isaaman, former Editor of the Hampstead and Highgate Express, Hampstead 'is not so much a place as a state of mind'. Wikipedia lists biographies of 201 Hampstead residents. Of these 130 were involved in one or other branch of the arts and only two in business.

The Everyman cinema

6 If that state of mind is one which admires education and taste rather than the accumulation of material possessions it helps to have money if you want to live in Hampstead. This is evidenced by the windows of four **estate agents** on this part of Heath Street, each of them selling homes in 2012 priced at £4 million or more.

7 By contrast, were you filming Dickens, the tenements and Victorian gas lamp in **Yorkshire Grey Yard** could present a good location.

Yorkshire Grey Yard

8 As you can see from the lettering above it, the premises Tesco now occupies originally belonged to the **Express Dairy Company**. The flats above the next parade have excellent detailed terracotta brickwork, recently restored. One section indicates its date, 1888, the year this section of Heath Street was constructed to link upper Heath Street with the recently constructed Fitzjohns Avenue.

The former premises of the Express Dairy Company

9 The date 1889 appears on the foundation stone of the **Hampstead Liberal Club** on the opposite side of the road.

10 From Heath Street turn right into **Church Row**. Church Row is Hampstead's finest street, little altered since the early 18th century when wealthy merchants built fine brick houses in Georgian style on both sides of a street wide enough to feel like a square.

Old and new lamp standards: Entrance to Church Row

11 At the corner of Heath Street and Church Row is an elaborate **lamp holder**. One can appreciate the efforts of Camden Council to replicate its style in its newer lamps.

12 Note the use of weatherboarding at No 5 Church Row, a practice common in villages in South East England. The decorative detail of the Georgian houses is restrained, focusing on the doors and their fanlights, the iron railings, the gates and the lamp brackets, most of which are **originals**. So too is much of the street's York stone paving.

Decorative iron work and door surround: Church Row

Famous former residents include at No 27 the cartoonist and author George du Maurier (1834 – 1896) whose work introduced the notions of "bedside manner" and "curate's egg" and at No 17 the science fiction writer and Socialist H G Wells (1866 – 1946).

13 Church Row is enclosed at the far end by **St John's Church**, built between 1745 and 1747. The iron gates of the main churchyard were brought from Canon's Park, Edgware at the time Handel was organist there. Why are the gates known as the Handel gates? Maybe they commemorate his playing the organ at their consecration.

St John's Church and Church Row: Painting by Gillian Lawson

As might be expected of a Hampstead churchyard, St John's contains tombs of many illustrious people, including **John Constable** and the clockmaker **John Harrison**.

14 On the opposite side of Church Road is the cemetery extension. Visible from the road and without entering the cemetery are inscriptions on memorials to George du Maurier and to Hugh Gaitskell, one of four former **leaders of the Labour Party** to have made their homes in Hampstead or its Garden Suburb.

15 Opposite the entrance to the church turn right up Holly Walk, past the churchyard extension. **Artists** attracted to the houses leading off this walk include the actress Dame Judi Dench, who lived in Prospect Place, which you pass shortly on your right, and Sir William Walton, composer of the March at the Queen's coronation in 1953, who lived in Hollyberry Lane, also on the right but further up the hill.

16 Shortly on your right you come to **St Mary's**, one of England's oldest Roman Catholic churches, built in 1816. The unusually narrow frontage was designed to conceal its existence. The church broadens out once you are inside. The façade was added only when Catholic worship had been accepted. Note the diagram above the entrance explaining the composition of the trinity.

Charles de Gaulle made the short journey from his home in Frognal to attend mass here during World War II.

17 **Moreton**, at the top of Holly Walk, was a much grander house before its garden was sold for the development of the contemporary house below it, concealed from pedestrian view by high walls. An early exemplar of the Arts and Crafts idiom, it is designed in the style of a 17th century manor house. Although its façade incorporates a statue of the Virgin Mary and theological inscriptions and its interior a private chapel, it has no connection with St Mary's.

Moreton, Holly Walk

Its exterior is one of few in Hampstead to be faced with pebble dash. Note at the rear the decorative hoppers that collect water from the roof. At one time it was used as an orphanage and at another as a nursing home.

18 No 9, the Watch House, was Hampstead's earliest **police station**.

19 At the top of Holly Walk you come to one of many pedestrian pathways in Hampstead, too steep and too narrow to be turned into roads. Bear right into **Mount Vernon**. The Georgian houses retain beautifully crafted fanlights above their front doors.

20 Above No 7, where Robert Louis Stevenson once lodged, you can see a rare example of a **Victorian gas lamp** for illuminating the front door with the house number

Gas light outside 7 Mount Vernon

etched on the lantern. Outside No 6 you can still see a plate which certified to the local fire brigade that the building was insured against fire.

21 At the top of Mount Vernon follow the road round the sharp bend to the left past the blue plaque to Sir Henry Dale, a Nobel prize-winning physiologist, and down to Holly Hill. On your left you will see what, when built in 1880, was the North London **Hospital for Consumption**. More recently it has been converted to luxury flats many of which currently accommodate Arsenal footballers.

22 Cross over into Holly Mount. This vehicular cul de sac leads onto a promontory whose residents obtain wonderful **views** of Central London across Hampstead rooftops. The houses are all of different styles, sizes and periods, the earliest dating from the reign of Queen Anne (1702 – 1714). Note at the end of Holly Mount the steps that take you down to Heath Street below. The Holly Bush Tavern exemplifies all that one would expect of an English public house.

The Holly Bush Tavern

Interior, Holly Bush Tavern

23 Many houses on Holly Mount retain examples of **old iron work**. An original boot scraper can be seen outside No 3. An original cast iron vent still survives between the ground and first floors. On the upper walls are braces of various designs to stop them bowing outwards. Just round the corner opposite the Holly Bush Tavern is an interesting old bell below which is recorded

"Tradesman's Entrance". Look carefully at the bell itself and you will see from where the word "servants" is embossed that it has been installed upside down.

"Upside down" door bell installation, Holly Mount

24 Returning to the entrance to Holly Mount, you will see across the junction with Holly Hill a splendid terrace of tall houses dating from the 1730s. Bear right and right again up Holly Bush Hill. Most the houses date from the 18th century. **Romney's House** was named after the 18th century painter and was more recently the home of the architect Clough Williams-Ellis, the creator of the Italianate tourist village of Portmeirion in North Wales.

25 A number of flights of **steps** enable pedestrians to drop down to the shops in Heath Street below. They also provide glimpses of the view across London to the east. This elevated position once supported a windmill.

26 **Fenton House** is one of the oldest buildings in Hampstead, dating from 1693. It houses a world-class collection of decorative and fine art, amassed by a host of eccentric collectors. Its panelled rooms display collections of ceramics,

Fenton House

needlework, furniture and paintings by the Camden Town Group of artists and musical instruments, ranging from the 15th to 19th centuries, which are still played regularly. Owned by The National Trust it is open between 11.00 and 17.00 between March and the end of October.

Entered through fine wrought iron gates Fenton House has a walled garden featuring a formal garden, rose garden, 300-year-old orchard and kitchen garden.

27 The turreted house at 28 Hampstead Grove was once the home of **George du Maurier**.

Admiral's House

28 Turn left into Admiral's Walk dominated by **Admiral's House**, a tall white building which appears to look out to sea. One of its more illustrious residents was Sir George Gilbert Scott Senior, designer of the Foreign & Commonwealth Office, Whitehall, the Albert Memorial and the recently restored St Pancras Station and Hotel.

29 Attached to it at the far end is **Grove Lodge**, the London home of the author of the Forsyte Saga, novelist and playwright John Galsworthy (1867 – 1933). It is where he died.

Home of John Constable, Lower Terrace

30 Where Admiral's Walk joins Lower Terrace look out for the terraced house at No 2 which **John Constable** rented for a few summers.

31 Before crossing over into Windmill Hill look behind you and you will see an excellent surviving example of a **Victorian letter box**.

32 Nearby is what is believed to be Hampstead's last surviving example of a Victorian lamp post with an original **ladder bar**. The bar, which protrudes 18 inches from the post, allowed a ladder to be attached to the post when the lantern required attention.

Victorian letter box

Original ladder bar

33 Upper Terrace in front of you is a row of mid-18th century houses with mansard roofs. To their left No 5, designed by Rick Mather and completed in 1997, is an example of modern design that has found favour with both the Heath & Hampstead Society and **architectural awards panels**.

34 The network of streets in this part of the Hampstead Heritage Trail is much more intricate than it is in sections A and B of the Trail either side of Belsize Park. This is because houses in this part of Hampstead were built piecemeal on what was previously **common land**, whereas the streets of Belsize were built by speculative developers seeking to maximise the number of homes they could fit on land bought from local landowners.

35 At the far end of Windmill Hill on the left is **Capo di Monte**, an ornamented rustic cottage with huge views out to the west. An early occupant, the actress Sarah Siddons, is one of many thousands who have sought improvements to their health from Hampstead's airy elevation and well drained sandy soil. Lord Clark, the art historian and broadcaster, and the critic and broadcaster Marghanita Laski are among Capo di Monte's former residents.

Capo di Monte

36 The distant views and fiery cloudscapes attracted the painter **John Constable** to use this part of the Heath as a setting for many of his most memorable paintings, notably westwards to **Harrow on the Hill**, whilst he lived in Lower Terrace. Its exposure to wild weather and openness to the clouds appealed particularly to his Romantic sensibility.

Hampstead Heath, looking towards Harrow 1821, John Constable

37 The extraction of sand for use in mortar explains the **steep hollow** immediately in front of Capo di Monte.

Judges Walk

38 Continue to your right along Judges Walk. The street sign is constructed from **ceramic tiles** of each letter, a practice which, in London at least, occurs only in the former borough of Hampstead. At the far end of Judges Walk you will see a plastic street sign designed to give the appearance of being constructed from these tiles.

39 Leaving Judges Walk, you have to bear slightly left and cross Lower Terrace into Hampstead Grove where on your right you will find a covered reservoir below an **astronomical observatory**.

40 Very shortly Whitestone Pond will come into view, at 440 feet the highest point in inner London. Old photographs show families visiting the Pond on outings and their children sailing boats on it. The pond was an important landmark on the coaching route between Hampstead and St Albans and until recently had extensive views south-eastwards over London as well as westwards. The "**white stone**" refers to a mile stone, visible on the left side of the path just before you cross West Heath Road.

Mile stone, Whitestone Pond

41 Close by the stone is a tree planted to celebrate the 50th anniversary of the United Nations.

Whitestone Pond at the turn of the 20th century

42 In 2010, following the inspiration and leadership of **The Heath & Hampstead Society**, the pond and its surrounds were restored to their original shape by Camden Council and English Heritage using granite and York stone. The filtration system and reed bed keep the water clean and prevent the growth of algae.

The ramp allowed the pond to be used by the horses of the Kings Troop which until 2012 rode here from their base in St John's Wood.

Whitestone Pond, 2010

43 In the 16th century, when views were less impeded by trees and houses, the site was an important link in a network of **beacons** used for giving advance warning of enemy attack, for example by the **Spanish Armada**. The beacon was located where the flagstaff now stands.

44 As late as the 17th century the crossing of this section of the Heath could be made hazardous by **highway robbers**. Close to the current flagstaff was a gibbet on which the bodies of robbers were hung as a deterrent.

45 Beyond Whitestone Pond is the weatherboarded **Jack Straw's Castle**. There was no "Jack Straw", this being a generic name used to describe a farm worker. The current building dates only from 1962. It was formerly a pub, an inn having stood on this spot since the 16th century. The space around the pub was licensed for bowls in the 17th century. **Charles Dickens** is said to have read his manuscripts in the inn.

A light-hearted re-invention of 18th century style, its creator was **Raymond Erith** (1904 -1973). His chief claim to distinction is his restoration of 10 and 11 Downing Street during Harold Macmillan's premiership.

Jack Straw's Castle

46 You might wonder why a coaching route should climb the highest point in inner London, Whitestone Pond, rather than detour round it. By keeping to **watersheds** these routes reduced the need to cross streams and boggy ravines. Equally important in the days before highway engineering, the risk of carriages **toppling over** was less on routes that avoided running along the sides of hills.

47 Opposite Jack Straw's Castle, behind a war memorial, is **Heath House**, the highest house in inner London. It was for many years owned by the Quaker anti-slavery campaigner Samuel Hoare. He and his descendents were members of a banking company that still survives under Hoare's name.

Points of interest: Whitestone Pond to Sunshine Corner

View across London from above the Vale of Health

48 Keeping Heath House to your left continue along Spaniards Road. To your right is an avenue of **pine trees** through which you can enjoy a most attractive view across the City.

Below these trees is one of a number of very ancient hamlets which developed around the Heath, the **Vale of Health**. Formerly known as Hatch's Bottom, it was renamed when a swampy piece of land was drained and turned into a small lake in 1777.

The Vale of Health from its pond

The Vale of Health was a favoured destination for the romantic poets of the early 19th century. This was due both to the wild and natural environment that encircled it and to it being the home between 1816 and 1821 of **Leigh Hunt** (1784-1859), an influential figure in the Romantic Movement and friend of Byron, Shelley and Keats. **D H Lawrence** also lived here for a while.

49 Walk along the left side of Spaniards Road as far as the bus shelter (M). Continue along the footpath between the road and the wall of Heath House until its end. You are now on the section of Hampstead Heath known as **Sandy Heath**. Drop down diagonally to your left along a curving footpath – not the one running beside the wall. You will come shortly to a grassy opening. Bear to the right and then, quite soon after and as you come to some gorse bushes, bear upwards to your left.

Pathway between gorse bushes

50 Maintenance of Hampstead Heath is the responsibility of the City of London. They manage this area using **coppice rotation** to create a mosaic of different vegetation heights. This provides a variety of nesting conditions and prevents woodland encroachment.

51 Note how fallen trees are **left to rot**, thereby providing a habitat for beetles and other forms of insect life.

52 The large area of gorse that can be found here provides a good habitat for **nesting birds** such as long tailed tits.

53 You will shortly see to your left the first of four **small ponds**. It is one of the best ponds on the heath for frogs due to its well vegetated and shallow nature.

54 The undulating landscape is the result of the thick beds of **Bagshot sand** that cover the highest section of Hampstead Heath. The sand was excavated during the second half of the 19th century for use in the mortar needed for laying bricks. During war time it was used to fill sand-bags. When this part of the Heath entered public ownership in 1889 these excavations had reduced the landscape to one of total despoliation.

Sand-digging on Sandy Heath, 1867. To the right is Spaniards Road

55 Evidence of the depth of working may be seen by comparing the level of the land with that of the roadway, Spaniards Road, which you can at times see to your right. It is also evident in places where the base of **ancient oaks** stands more than a metre above the surrounding land, their roots still clearly visible.

300 year oaks on Sandy Heath

56 How ponds survive in such a sandy environment may seem strange since they are not fed by springs nor do they drain anywhere. The explanation is that the sandy Bagshot Beds contain deposits of iron which when soaked in water oxidise and cause the sand to coalesce into an impermeable sandstone layer known as **iron pan**.

Though the discolouration caused by the iron gives the appearance of pollution these ponds support distinctive and thriving eco systems. They support a population of smooth newts and rudd. A heron can often be found fishing and as many as 40 **mandarin duck** have been known to overwinter.

A heron beside the third iron pan pond

57 Beyond the third and largest pond, where you find a bench in memory of Barbara Myers, is Sandy Road, a former **roadway** which linked Highgate Village to North End. At this point turn left, following the path as it curves downhill, bearing left on to the asphalt and then along a lane to a cross roads marking the settlement of North End.

58 North End is one of a number of settlements which grew up on the common land that surrounded Hampstead Heath to house **landless commoners**. Their economic status

The Old Bull and Bush

was very different to that of today's residents of these rural enclaves.

59 Since you have now reached the half way point of this section you might like to drink or eat at the **Old Bull and Bush**, dating from 1721 and immortalised in the old music hall song "Down at the Old Bull and Bush". If so continue straight down North End for eighty yards, otherwise turn right at the cross roads where North End meets North End Avenue.

60 Shortly on your right you will find the home of Michael Ventris (1922 – 1956), an architect and classical scholar who played a major role in the deciphering of the Cretan script **Linear B** before his death in a car accident.

61 The unmade road curves to the right just before Wyldes where No 2 Wildwood Terrace was once the home of the architectural historian **Nikolaus Pevsner** (1902 – 1983), celebrated for his compilation of a 46-volume series of county-by-county guides, The Buildings of England.

Home of Nikolaus Pevsner

62 You soon come to **Wyldes**, a weatherboarded house dating from the 17th century.

For many years it was the home of the landscape painter John Linnell (1792 – 1882), a contemporary and rival of John Constable and friend and patron of William Blake, a frequent visitor to the house. **Dickens** is another who sought solace in its rustic charm. It was to Wyldes that he came to recover from the death of his sister-in-law Mary Hogarth and his wife's miscarriage.

It was later home to Mrs Charlotte Wilson, an early Fabian Socialist, who organised the Hampstead Historic Club and whose circle included George Bernard Shaw and Sydney Webb.

Wyldes

63 In the 1890s an American railway magnate, Charles Yerkes, developed plans to extend the Northern Line from Hampstead to Golders Green. This incorporated an underground station at Wildwood Terrace to serve North End. As a result of overhearing these plans when they were fellow passengers on a voyage to Russia in 1896, **Dame Henrietta Barnett** (1851 – 1936), philanthropist and resident of Heath End at the Highgate end of Sandy Road, campaigned to raise money to purchase Wyldes Farm and 80 acres of land from its owners, the Eton College Estate. Her purpose was to protect the land from the sort of suburban development which typically sprung up around new tube stations.

The original 80 acres stretched the whole width of the farm but unable to raise the full price the campaign team made an offer for a new shape, still 80 acres but longer and thinner at a significantly lower price, the Eton Estate being compensated by the **increased development value** of the unsold land fronting the open space.

The purchase of this land, which became known as the Heath Extension, made the station no longer viable and, although the platforms had been built, and can still be seen from passing trains between Golders Green and Hampstead, the station was **never opened**.

By co-incidence Wyldes Farm had originally been granted to Eton College by the Crown at the same time as the **Eton Estate** covered in **B** 40.

64 During her husband Canon Samuel Barnett's time as the first warden of Toynbee Hall in London's East End, Henrietta Barnett became one of the country's leading protagonists in campaigns to improve the conditions of the "industrial classes". Through her detailed knowledge of social conditions and her flair for publicity and fund raising for philanthropic causes, she created a remarkable network of contacts in high places. This subsequently enabled her to mobilise support and funds for her vision of a **Garden Suburb** on additional land, also acquired from the Eton College Estate, either side of the Heath Extension and beyond it as far as Temple Fortune and East Finchley.

The architect and town planner chosen by Henrietta Barnett to plan and design what became Hampstead Garden Suburb, **Raymond Unwin** (1863 – 1940), lived

Henrietta Barnett aged eighty: Portrait by Maurice Codner

at Wyldes when he was appointed by Henrietta Barnett in 1906 and converted the barn into a drawing office.

65 Beyond Wyldes the pathway drops down to **Wildwood Road**. At this point the juxtaposition of acid heath and fertile pasture and of steep and gentle slopes indicates you are crossing from Bagshot Sand to Claygate Beds.

66 Cross the road past an ancient oak and, crossing a horse riding track, continue along an avenue of beeches. Beyond them is the grazing land that formerly belonged to Wyldes Farm. Gifted in 1907 to the London County Council, the **Heath Extension** is now managed by the City of London Corporation.

From this point and others further on you may be able to see the spire of the parish church of **St Jude-on-the-Hill**, the landmark building at the centre of Hampstead Garden Suburb. You can see that land on either side of the Heath Extension was developed with houses for the rich, built around this narrow rectangular space, to support affordable cottages in the Artisan Quarter at the north western end of the Suburb. The Extension provides a vista of St Jude's and connects the Suburb to the Heath with a green corridor.

67 Walk down the path ahead of you as far as a **Grecian fountain**. The

The Grecian fountain

fountain was erected by his sister Emily to commemorate the water colourist Walter Field (1837 – 1901). Emily was at the time secretary of the Hampstead Heath Protection Society and a co-campaigner with Henrietta Barnett. Her brother lived at the Pryors (see Ⓐ 37).

68 At this point bear off through the trees to your right on a small path which very shortly crosses a dip between the second and a series of five other ponds. Then keep bearing to the left along the perimeter fence of a **wildlife reserve**. The ponds are managed by the City of London's Hampstead Heath team and are home to kingfishers and many species of duck.

Mandarin duck: Heath Extension lower pond

69 When you come to an open field level with the last of the ponds take a track to your left. Shortly, where paths cross, you will see in the field above and to your left a **playground** suitable for the very young. The field containing the playground had, until 1939, served as a pen within which to keep the sheep that grazed on the Heath Extension.

At this cross roads turn right on to a broad pathway downhill in the direction of the spire of St Jude's. This pathway was once the main route between Hampstead and Hendon. The **veteran oaks** hereabouts form part of the ancient hedgerows delineating the boundaries of the fields dating from when forests were cleared here in the 16th century.

70 To your left you will see tall buildings with even **taller chimneys** silhouetted against the sky. This is Heathcroft, a large block of mansion flats developed in the 1920s for middle class families who liked the convenience of apartment living. In the distance you may be able to see the hills above Harrow which the M1 crosses beyond London Gateway Services.

St Jude's from the Hampstead Heath Extension

71 Further on you come to some buildings which are now used as a store and workshop by the City of London and as changing rooms. The complex houses **public conveniences**. Below this point, in Barn Field, a gunnery defended Golders Green during World War II.

72 It may be possible to make out on the upper storeys of the houses to your left **white wooden balconies**. These were designed for summer outdoor sleeping, at a time when fresh air was considered as critical to health as healthy eating is now.

Sleeping balcony, 67 Hampstead Way

73 At this point the going underfoot may become muddy after recent rain as you cross from sandy Claygate Beds to London clay. Keep to the right between the **cricket ground** and its practice nets, close to the hedgerow which points in the direction of St Jude's spire. Passing a number of field boundaries you come to a small brook. Cross this on a wooden bridge into Bush field used in winter as a Rugby pitch.

74 Ahead of you is a series of towers which gives the appearance of defensive look outs. These **gazebos**, and the wall that links them, were an important part of Hampstead Garden Suburb's design. They are owned by properties fronting the Heath Extension and each incorporates a fireplace as well as a private gate to the Heath.

Influenced by visits to Bavarian hill towns, Unwin and his colleagues saw the "**Great Wall**" as delineating the boundary between the Suburb and surrounding countryside, an edge which defined and gave coherence to the settlement.

Work on the Great Wall was ended by World War I by when less than a half of the original planned length had been completed.

Gazebo on the Great Wall at Sunshine Corner

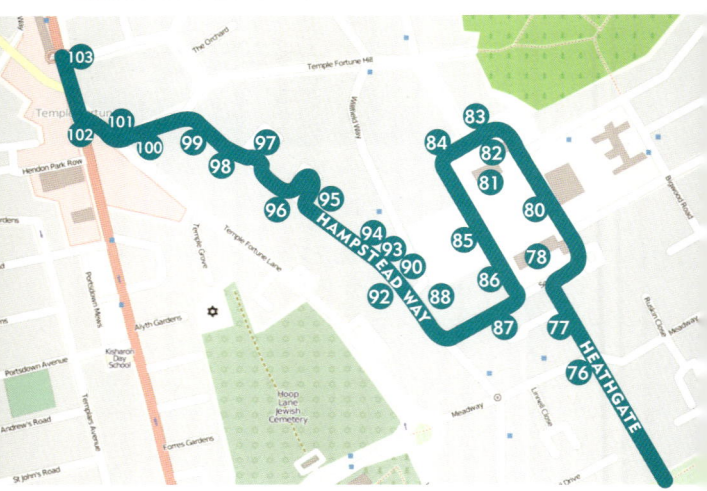

Points of interest: Sunshine Corner to Temple Fortune

75 The steps at the recently restored Sunshine Corner lead you up to Heathgate which ends at South Square, the first of three squares that form the focal centre of the Suburb. Heathgate starts with large detached and semi detached houses in the **Georgian Revival** style, built from 1907 until the 1920s.

76 The intersection of Heathgate and Meadway is a good example of a "**dog leg**" offset junction, a technique commonly used by the Suburb's designers to create a sense of enclosure, a reaction against the monumentalism striven for in the late 19th century road layouts as for example in Haussmann's Parisian boulevards.

77 Beyond Meadway Heathgate consists of terraced houses built in a soft grey brick with red detailing.

Neo-Georgian Heathgate

Heathgate's appearance was strongly influenced by the ideas of the architect **Edwin Lutyens** (1869 – 1924), at that time Britain's leading designer of country houses. Henrietta Barnett had engaged Lutyens to work both on St Jude-on-the-Hill and the overall layout of the Suburb's three focal squares. A recurring feature of Lutyens's work is the imaginative use of traditional English building forms and materials often within the framework of Arts and Crafts design. Later in his career, when it was decided that New Delhi should become the new capital of India, Lutyens was asked to oversee the plans for its development.

78 With its hill top location and 178 foot spire St Jude's church is a landmark visible from most parts of the Suburb and many places beyond. Executed in Byzantine style, building began in 1909. Though the church was consecrated in 1911 it was not completed until 1935. Simon Jenkins, in his Companion Guide to Outer London, describes it as Lutyens's "**ecclesiastical masterpiece**" and "one of the best 20th century church exteriors in England".

St Jude's-on-the-Hill

The church takes its name from St Jude's church in Whitechapel where Canon Samuel Barnett, husband of Henrietta Barnett, was vicar. Saint Jude is depicted in the west window, with a cross in his right hand and this church in his left. Below is his symbol, the ship, above, Christ in glory, surrounded by the traditional symbols of the four evangelists.

A memorial to the **horses** killed in World War I is situated on the north side of the west door. On the south wall is a memorial to Edward VII.

Each June a music festival **Proms at St Jude's** is held at the church. Concerts and guided walks raise funds for the North London Hospice and Toynbee Hall where Canon Barnett used to be the Warden.

79 Unlike most village centres, Lutyens' plans for the Suburb's centre, unlike Unwin's earlier proposals which they replaced, included neither **shops** nor offices. By contrast the Squares have three places of worship and one school.

80 From South Square, continue anti-clockwise around Central Square passing the Vicarage and Southway, where Harold Wilson once lived, to the former **Institute**, now **The Henrietta Barnett School for Girls**.

Her concern for the better education of girls resulted in the founding by Dame Henrietta Barnett of a predecessor to the school in 1911. At a time when the most of the Suburb's residents were less well off than they are today, it was Dame Henrietta's belief that girls should be educated on the basis of their **natural ability**, not the financial status of their parents.

Licence above doorway at The Institute

The central building, **The Institute**, designed by Sir Edwin Lutyens and John Soutar, was part of the overall design for Central Square. Originally intended as an adult education centre for concerts, evening classes and debates, but nonetheless also licensed for music and dancing, during the day the Institute was, latterly, given over to the Henrietta Barnett School for Girls which opened on the site in the 1930s.

Glass panel above the entrance to what is now Henrietta Barnett School

As a result of conflicts between the School and the Institute over shared use of the building, the Institute vacated the entire site and **relocated** to East Finchley in 2004.

In 2011 the school commissioned Hopkins Architects to develop two **new blocks**, one for the teaching of Music and Drama and the other for Design, Technology and Art. These buildings are two of the largest buildings added to the Suburb since 1945.

The Free Church, Central Square

81 Beyond the school, in and around North Square, is the Hampstead Garden Suburb **Free Church**, its church hall, accessed from Northway, and a Manse. The Suburb planners also made provision on the corner of North Square for a meeting house for the Quaker Society of Friends funded by the Cadburys and designed by a Rowntree.

The Free Church was controversial in its time for serving the needs of all non-conformist denominations. Its inscription, "**God is larger than the creeds**", was selected by Henrietta Barnett and obtained the approval of Queen Mary, an early backer of Dame Henrietta's vision of the Garden Suburb and a frequent visitor to it.

82 Note the **yew hedges**. The use of hedges to separate front gardens from the street is a trademark feature of the Garden Suburb. South Square hedges are beech, others are of privet and hornbeam.

83 Nos 9 – 16 North Square is a terrace of three-storey houses designed by Lutyens between 1907 and 1910. The dormers are a mix of timber sliding sashes and metal casement windows. The fanlights above their front doors are in varying styles. No 9 incorporates a black and white **wooden sundial**, with roman numerals and metal pointer on a raised rectangular plaque with quotation and date, 1920. No 12 is the house Henrietta Barnett first moved to on the death of her husband, Canon Samuel Barnett, in 1913. Their previous home was in the cloisters of Westminster Abbey.

Blind niches and balustraded balconies, North Square

(84) The next terrace follows Lutyens' style, the greyish brick contrasting with the red quoins and bays. Despite the overall consistency of the design, North Square exemplifies the care architects took throughout the Suburb to give each house its own **distinctive features**, for example using projecting bays and dormers, balustraded balconies, blind niches and fine door surrounds.

Memorial to Henrietta Barnett, framing The Institute

85 On the west side of St Jude's is a **memorial** incorporating a metal arch and a stone laurel wreath dedicated to the memory of Henrietta Barnett.

86 Continue on into South Square past No 1, the house to which Henrietta Barnett moved from North Square in 1915. The house immediately beyond has an unusual **double row of dormers**.

87 Turn right into a pedestrian pathway, locally referred to as a "twitten", leading to Hill Close.

Double row of dormers, South Square

At this point you move from the neo-Georgian classical grandeur of Lutyens to the Arts and Crafts informality of Unwin.

Hill Close is one of many occurrences in the Suburb of a **close**, a device the Suburb's planners held to be an effective means of fostering community. This is just one of many elements of the Suburb's layout that had a major influence on the design of social and private sector housing between the wars. At the foot of Hill Close turn right into Hampstead Way.

88 The design of the junction with Willifield Way is testimony to the influence on Unwin of the Italian urban theorist Camillo Sitte, an advocate of irregular house lines to create enclosure. A former hedge row is used to form the edge of one of the Suburb's many small public spaces.

89 You have now entered one of the earliest parts of the Suburb where the layout of the roads, the overall design of the houses and much of their detail was the work of Unwin's own team

Doors and Windows

Hampstead Way

of architects. The design of Hampstead Way exemplified the belief of Henrietta Barnett that the Suburb should cater for a **cross section** of different income groups and family circumstances.

90 Nos 42 - 54 on the right, eastern, side of the road are raised above the level of the road from which, unusually for the Suburb, they are separated by retaining walls rather than hedges. This gives variety and an **open aspect** to this side of the road.

91 The houses on the left side, dating from around 1908, are typical of the **Arts and Crafts** style of the older part of the Suburb. The style features steeply pitched roofs, roofs with dormer windows, two storey bay windows and gables.

A guiding principle of the Suburb's founders was to house people in a pleasant environment in well designed homes with access to fresh air and attractive landscapes. This was Unwin's response to the de-humanising effects of the **Industrial Revolution** with its emphasis on standardisation and techniques of mass production. Dignity was to be recovered by a re-connection with nature and by the use of quality craftsmanship in dwellings each with their distinct appearance.

The Arts and Crafts style meshed with this philosophy with its revival of **vernacular** building forms which prevailed in Medieval Britain, with its delight in the informality of **rural** building styles and with its preference for **traditional** materials rather than surface ornamentation.

163 Hampstead Way

92 No 163 provides a good example of Arts and Crafts design with its full height canted bay with hipped roof, tiled porch and red brick pattern on the chimney. The stair tower is evocative of a **Medieval turret**. With the other half of the pair having been designed by a different architect, the building is a good example of the interest among the Suburb's architects in asymmetrical, picturesque designs.

46 Hampstead Way

93 Likewise No 46, which was built by T M Wilson, a Trust architect, for his own use, is another house distinguished by a deliberately asymmetrical gable containing a **porthole window**. It is covered in smooth white plaster and its bay has a roundel containing a flower vase. Features such as this differentiated Suburb houses from the standardised output of London's speculative builders.

48 Hampstead Way

94 Most of the houses in the Suburb, whilst showing individual features, nevertheless conform to design themes that were consistent within their road. No 48, designed by Barry Parker, is an example, uncommon in the older Suburb, of a one-off design. Note how a **continuous canopy** crosses the entire front of the house, windows and doors, a practice that was to become common in London houses in the 1920s and 1930s.

Lucas Square

95 Lucas Square, Nos 60-82 Hampstead Way, was built by Geoffry Lucas round a green, formerly used as a tennis court, separated from the road by a high red brick wall. The Suburb's founders attached great importance to the preservation of a rural setting, retaining old trees and **hedge lines** wherever possible. The four oaks beside the road explain why Lucas Square is set back from it.

The tall chimney stacks, such a prominent feature in Lucas Square, are strongly characteristic of the Arts and Crafts style. They are made more prominent by being set into the front elevations and built in brick to contrast with the roughly surfaced houses. Two such stacks form the **central feature** of the square where they are used to frame an oriel window above a gated twitten.

195 Hampstead Way

96 Nos 195-199 form an unusual terrace of three houses, rendered with a long tiled roof and deep eaves. Their two bays are capped with hipped tiled roofs which echo the towers at the entrances to the Suburb at Sunshine Corner (see **74**), at Temple Fortune (see **103**) and in the Market Place (see **D** 53).

97 Like Lucas Square, **Litchfield Square**, built by Parker and Unwin in 1908, owes its layout to Unwin's affection for the quadrangle as an element of residential layout. It also illustrates the attempt by Unwin's team to add variety through the use of different types of brick, in this case brown bricks with red arches. Attention is attracted to the façades by the tiled, conical roofs above the bay projections. Its name commemorates the Trust's secretary.

Early postcard of Litchfield Square

As is common throughout the Suburb subtle differences abound. Whereas most of the Square's houses have a recessed porch, five houses have front doors set flush with the front façade. All but two doors retain their original **stained glass** panels.

The large trees towering over the roofs contribute to the rustic charm as do the two limes at the entrances to the Square.

Art Nouveau stained glass panelled door, Litchfield Square

98 Worth noting towards the end of this section of Hampstead Way is No 215, with its charming hipped, tiled dormers, and windows with leaded lights. Another house designed by an architect for his own use, it is set **sideways** to the road.

99 Nos 219 and 221 attract the eye with their brick staircase bays which extend above the upper floor creating the appearance of a **turret**.

100 At the corner bear left into Farm Walk past one of the many tennis courts that provided recreation to Suburb pioneers. See booklet **D** for more information on Queen's Court to your right. Don't overlook Nos 3-5, organised to create the outward appearance of a **Medieval manor house**.

Doorway: Temple Fortune Court

101 Turn right into Temple Fortune Lane past **Temple Fortune Court**, with its steep tiled roof, chimneys and classical stone door surrounds, and right again when you reach Finchley Road.

102 Finchley Road was cut in 1827 to connect London's West End with North Finchley where it joins the principal coaching route from the City to the North of England. The shopping parades at Temple Fortune were developed from 1910 onwards following the extension of the **Northern Line** to Golders Green in 1907 and the demand for suburban housing that this stimulated. The name Temple Fortune is believed to originate from the Knights Templar, who owned land here in the 13th century.

103 Much of the land to the east of the Finchley Road had been acquired between 1907 and 1911 by the Hampstead Garden Suburb Trust so it was logical to consider that one of the principal **entrances** to the Garden Suburb should be via Hampstead Way.

Arcade House and Temple Fortune House

Arcade House and **Temple Fortune House**, two imposing brick buildings whose German style must have been an arresting sight, rising up over the farmland before the surrounding buildings were developed. When they were built they served to provide a degree of monumentality to the entrance to the Suburb.

This is achieved by the use of stone arcades, the square brick "look-out" towers reminiscent of the pavilions along the Great Wall, protruding from a gabled roof-line, the exceptionally tall chimneys, the timber balconies and windows and the oak balustrades of the external staircases that give access to the flats above the shops. Their design was influenced by the architecture of **Rothenburg** in Bavaria.

Rothenburg, Bavaria

Further information

At **www.northernheights.eu** you can find out more about the Northern Heights Partnership, order other booklets and provide feedback.

More detailed information about Hampstead Village and Hampstead Garden Suburb can be found in:

Barnett, Dame Henrietta, The Story of the Growth of the Hampstead Garden Suburb, 1907 - 1928, 1928

Creedon, Alison, Only a Woman, 2006

Denford, Steven, The Hampstead Book: The A-Z of its history and people, 2009

Farmer, Alan, Hampstead Heath, 1984

Gray, Stuart, Edwardian Architecture, a biographical, 1985

Hampstead Garden Suburb Residents Association, Walking in Hampstead Garden Suburb – The Artisans' Quarter, 1998

Hampstead Garden Suburb Trust and London Borough of Barnet, Hampstead Garden Suburb Character Appraisal, 2010

McDowall, David and Wolton, Deborah, The Walkers Guide to Hampstead Heath, 2006

Miller, Mervyn, Hampstead Garden Suburb, Arts and Crafts Utopia?, 2006,

Slack, Kitty, Henrietta's Dream, 1982

Wade, Christopher, Hampstead Past, 2002

Watkins, Micky, Henrietta Barnett – social worker and community planner, 2011

© 2012 Heath & Hampstead Society and Hampstead Garden Suburb Trust

Series Editor: The Highgate Society

Publisher: Northern Heights Publications,
　　　　　　10a South Grove, London, N6 6BS

Distributor: www.northernheights.eu

Designer: Nicholas Moll Design

Printer: Rainbow Print Wales

A CIP catalogue record for this book is available from the British Library.

ISBN: 978-0-9572079-8-1

All rights reserved. No part of this publication may be reproduced, stored in a retrieval system, or transmitted in any form or by any means, electronic, mechanical, photocopying, recording or otherwise, without prior permission from the copyright owners.

Except where specifically acknowledged or where we have been unable to trace copyright, copyright of the photographs belongs to Northern Heights Publications. These can be reproduced under the provisions of the commons creative licence arrangement. Permission has been obtained for the reproduction of illustrations as follows: POI 13 Gillian Lawson, POI 41 Camden Local Studies and Archives Centre.

While every effort has been made by the publisher to ensure that the information contained in this guide is accurate and up to date as at the date of publication, they accept no responsibility or liability in contract, tort, negligence, breach of statutory duty or otherwise for any inconvenience, loss, damage, costs or expenses of any nature whatsoever incurred or suffered by anyone as a result of any advice or information contained in this guide (except to the extent that such liability may not be excluded or limited as a matter of law).

The Hampstead Garden Suburb Trust

The Hampstead Garden Suburb Trust is the successor to the company, founded by Dame Henrietta Barnett, which developed the Suburb from 1907 onwards. Any Suburb resident of three years' standing can become a Member of the Trust company. Newer residents can join as Associate Members. It costs nothing to become a member, and forms and further information can be found on our website **www.hgstrust.org**

The Trust is a registered charity charged with maintaining the character and amenity of the Suburb. Recognised worldwide as one of the most important utopian developments of the 19th and 20th centuries, Hampstead Garden Suburb was carefully designed in terms of architecture, landscape and town planning. The Trust has a legal obligation to uphold certain standards, and has to strike a balance between accepting change and conserving character. It has an important role to play in fostering good design and workmanship. The objective of the Trust is not to stop residents from altering their houses, but to ensure that changes are in keeping with the spirit of the original design.

People come to live on the Suburb because of the delightful houses and gardens, which have remained relatively unspoilt for over a century. By working closely with the Trust, the whole community benefits, so that in another hundred years there will still be a Suburb of which future generations can be proud.

=HAMPSTEAD · GARDEN · SVBVRB · TRVST=

The Heath & Hampstead Society

Since its foundation in 1897, the Heath & Hampstead Society has fought to safeguard Hampstead Heath as an oasis of unspoiled countryside in the heart of Europe's greatest metropolis.

We continue to fight for it today, to keep it open for all to use, free from signs telling us to keep out or keep off and free from traffic. We fight to retain it as a place for relaxation, enjoyment and peaceful contact with nature.

We consult closely with the City of London on all aspects of their management of the Heath and with English Heritage on matters relating to Kenwood.

Our activities include
- Conservation work
- The monitoring of biodiversity on the Heath
- Public guided walks covering flora, fauna and history

The Society also seeks to preserve and enhance Hampstead Village.

This involves opposing inappropriate developments but encouraging the best modern design where sites are available, refurbishing street furniture and supporting local business. We seek to preserve trees and get involved in issues that affect our members such as licensing, traffic, policing and the environment.

The Society has about 2,000 members from all walks of life. It makes no profits and depends entirely on volunteers. Thankfully those volunteers care deeply for the Heath and Hampstead, and bring a mix of skills, experience and local knowledge that money cannot buy. We are strictly non party-political and our members are represented by about 30 people sitting on a General Committee and four Sub-Committees - for the Heath, Town, Planning and the Web.

www.heathandhampstead.org.uk